The Human Body

The Digestive System

THE HUMAN BODY

Kristin Petrie MS, RD • ABDO Publishing Company

visit us at
www.abdopublishing.com

Printed in the United States.

Cover Photo: Corbis
Interior Photos: © Birmingham/Custom Medical Stock Photo p. 10; © BSIP/Custom Medical Stock Photo p. 7; Corbis pp. 6, 21, 25, 26, 29; Getty Images pp. 4, 5, 8, 9, 11, 12, 13, 15, 17, 18, 23; Visuals Unlimited p. 27

Series Coordinator: Heidi M. Dahmes
Editors: Rochelle Baltzer, Heidi M. Dahmes
Art Direction: Neil Klinepier

Library of Congress Cataloging-in-Publication Data

Petrie, Kristin, 1970-
    The digestive system / Kristin Petrie.
      p. cm. -- (The human body)
    Includes index.
    ISBN-10 1-59679-710-X
    ISBN-13 978-1-59679-710-9
    1. Digestive organs--Juvenile literature. 2. Gastrointestinal system--Juvenile literature. I. Title.

QP145.P457 2006
612.3--dc22
                                            2005048322

CONTENTS

FOOD IS ENERGY

Growl! Is that your stomach? Our bodies create some strange sounds. There are weird movements going on inside our bodies, too. What is happening in there? These sounds and movements come from your digestive system.

This noisy system turns the food you eat into substances your body can use. Luckily, you don't have to work hard or even think about digestion. All you have to do is eat. Your body will do the rest.

From the outside, the digestive system seems like a simple food tube. Your breakfast cereal enters the mouth. It

A meal takes 30 to 40 hours to travel the length of the digestive tract.

travels through the esophagus, the stomach, and the intestines. Easy, right?

On the other hand, that was a big bowl of cereal. You feel pretty full after eating it. However, soon it disappears. And, you forget about it as you run off to play. Where did all that cereal go? Where did all of your energy come from? Maybe the digestive system isn't so simple after all.

A healthy diet prevents you from getting certain illnesses. It also helps you heal from others.

YOUR HUNGRY BRAIN

Where does the digestive system start? This seems like a silly question. The mouth, of course! But, you could also say that the digestive system starts at your brain. The mere thought of your favorite food releases digestive juices. The sight or smell of this food makes the response even stronger.

Think back to the last time you passed a fast-food restaurant. You weren't hungry, but one whiff from the grill changed that. Your mouth started watering, and your stomach started growling.

The sense of smell is also known as olfaction. Odors come from molecules that are released in the air. Just the smell of food increases saliva flow in your mouth.

What now? You may have gone on your way and forgotten about eating. Your stomach did the same. Or, you stopped to refuel. In that case, your digestive system started working from the first bite.

Many different substances release molecules into the air. When these molecules enter your nose, they stimulate receptor cells. These cells send impulses to olfactory nerves. The nerves carry the impulses to the brain. Your brain then tells you what you are smelling.

THE MOUTH

Hello, burger! Your teeth say "welcome" and your taste buds say "thanks." Now starts a very important part of digestion, chewing.

Chewing breaks food into small pieces. This is important for a few reasons. First, chewing keeps you from choking on big pieces of food. And, smaller pieces of food are more easily broken down during the digestive process. Lastly, chewing helps spit, or saliva, reach all of the food in your mouth.

Like cars, our bodies need fuel in order to run. Food is the fuel for our bodies.

Saliva contains digestive juices. These juices break down some foods even before they leave your mouth. Saliva also moistens dry food.

The tongue is covered with small projections called papillae. Our taste buds are found inside the papillae. We have four kinds of taste buds. They allow us to tell the difference between sour, sweet, salty, and bitter tastes.

Your tongue also does a lot of work. Everyone knows that its taste buds help us taste our food. But, the tongue has several more jobs. It mixes food with saliva. It positions food to where your teeth can crush it. And, it forms food pieces into a ball. This is called a bolus.

One of your tongue's most important tasks is the least obvious. The tongue pushes the bolus to the back of your mouth. Then, the bolus enters your pharynx, or throat. Thanks to your tongue, you don't have to throw your head back to swallow!

THE THROAT AND THE EPIGLOTTIS

Once the bolus has entered your pharynx, its journey has only just begun! Pressure within your mouth and throat moves the bolus toward your esophagus.

But hold on. Your trachea, or windpipe, sits right behind your mouth. If you're not careful, food will go down the wrong tube! Luckily, a trapdoor closes off the windpipe when you swallow food or liquids. This smart flap is called the epiglottis. It makes sure food stays in your esophagus and doesn't slip into the air tube.

Pharynx

Salivary Glands

However, sometimes things don't go as planned. Food or liquid may sneak into your trachea. This causes you to cough **automatically**. Other times, you may swallow a bigger piece of food than planned. Hopefully you can cough to dislodge it from your throat. These problems happen more when you eat too fast. So, slow down and chew your food.

If a person is choking, he or she cannot breathe or talk. That individual will need help to remove the item that is stuck. The Heimlich maneuver forces objects out of the windpipe. If the item is not dislodged in four to six minutes, the person could die.

THE ESOPHAGUS

Have you ever seen a snake swallow its prey? Snakes have teeth, but most don't use them for chewing. Instead they swallow their food whole, and it moves down their stretchy bodies. The next part of your food tube is also very stretchy. It is called the esophagus, and it connects your throat to your stomach.

The esophagus is about ten inches (25 cm) long. It looks narrow, but it contracts and expands to move food to the stomach.

Thankfully, humans have teeth for chewing. We don't have to swallow our meals whole! Nevertheless, the esophagus is made of **elastic** muscular walls. The muscles work to move food and liquids through the esophagus at a steady rate. This **automatic** action is called peristalsis.

At the bottom of the esophagus, there is a muscular door. This **sphincter** regulates the entrance of food and liquid into your stomach. When peristaltic waves deliver food and liquid to it, the sphincter opens. This allows food and liquid to enter your stomach.

Your esophagus carries food from your throat to your stomach in about ten seconds.

THE STOMACH

You're very familiar with your stomach. Sometimes it's jumpy. Other times it's calm. Sometimes it's full, and other times it's empty. When it is really full, your stomach is about as large as a one-gallon (4-L) jug! When it is empty, it is no bigger than a fist.

The inside of your stomach is slimy and wrinkled. It has many folds. A thick layer of mucus coats it. Mucus protects the stomach's lining from its own strong hydrochloric acid. Cells in your stomach walls produce this acid.

Your stomach has two main jobs. The first is to temporarily hold your **ingested** food. The stomach holds food for up to five hours, depending on the type of food. For example, vegetables remain in the stomach for no longer than two hours. The stomach's next job is to mix and turn the food. This helps digestive juices and acids reach every morsel of food.

Gastric juices, which contain **enzymes** and hydrochloric acid, continue to break down your foods. When their job is complete, the result is a thick liquid called chyme.

The stomach holds food for several hours. For example, a meal of meat and potatoes remains in the stomach for a long period of time. This makes you feel full longer. Then, your stomach turns that meal into chyme.

THE SMALL INTESTINE

So, your stomach liquefied your food. Now it's time to move on. The next stop along the digestive tract is the small intestine. But, don't let the name fool you. This is the longest part of the digestive tract.

This intestine is called small because it is smaller in **diameter** than the large intestine. Still, if you stretched out your small intestine, it would be about 22 to 25 feet (7 to 8 m) long. That's longer than your parent's minivan!

This long tube is your body's main place for digestion and absorption. The top part of the small intestine is called the duodenum. This section is attached to your stomach by the pyloric **sphincter**. The pyloric sphincter opens to release chyme in spurts. This allows a small amount of the liquid to enter the duodenum.

Opposite page: The small intestine's surface area is more than 2,150 square feet (200 sq m). That is equal to the floor area of an average two-story house!

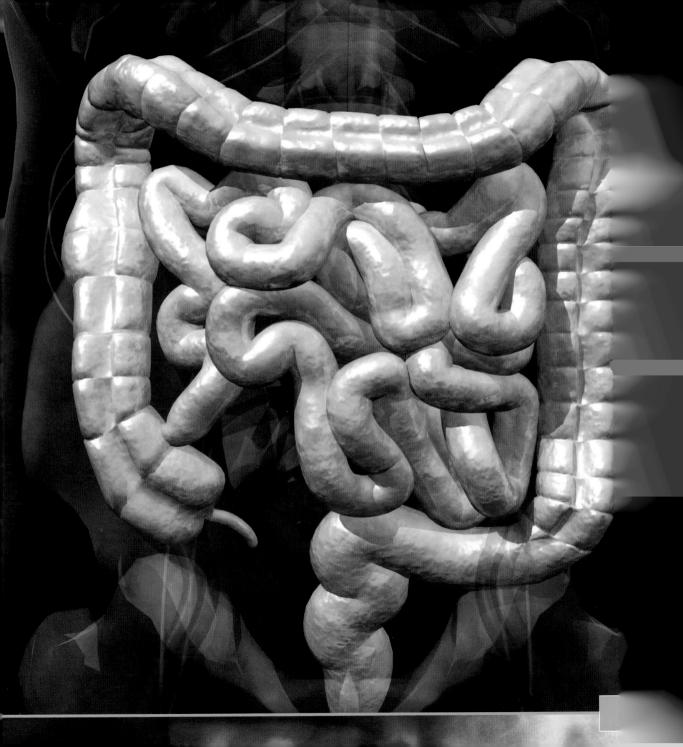

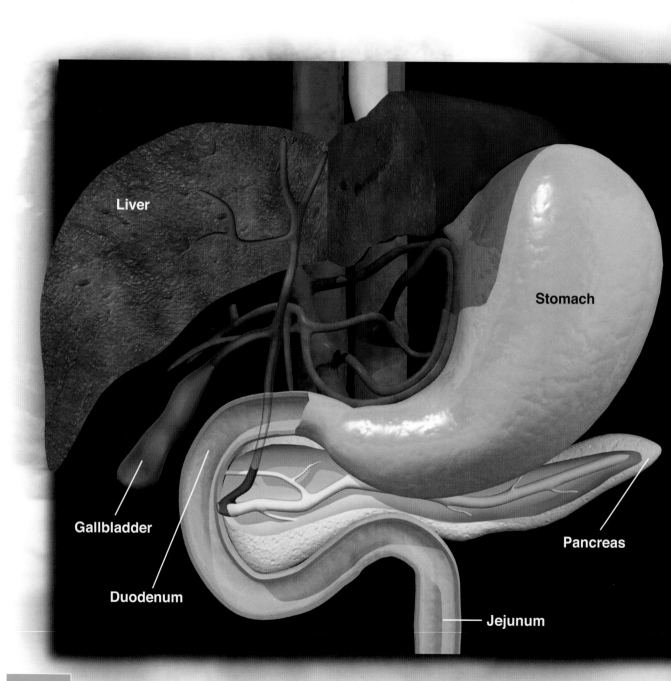

Liver

Stomach

Gallbladder

Pancreas

Duodenum

Jejunum

The duodenum is about ten inches (25 cm) long. It loops around the head of another digestive gland, the pancreas. When the duodenum receives the chyme, it sends **hormones** to the pancreas. In response, the pancreas releases more digestive juices.

Pancreatic juice contains special **enzymes**. Enzymes called amylase and maltase break down carbohydrates. An enzyme called trypsin breaks down proteins. And, a fourth enzyme called lipase breaks down fats.

Other **organs** get to work here, too. Your liver produces bile. This is a strong liquid that works with lipase to help digest fats. It is stored in the gallbladder, another organ, until fats are detected. Bile also helps absorb fats.

The duodenum is followed by the jejunum. The duodenum and the jejunum are the twisty-turny, coiled sections of your small intestine. The jejunum is followed by the last section, the ileum.

Tiny fingerlike projections called villi line all three parts of the small intestine. Each villus contains special cells and blood vessels. The cells grab **nutrients** as they pass through the small intestine. The blood vessels then transport the absorbed proteins and carbohydrates.

FOOD IN MY BLOOD?

That's right! After food particles have been broken down to their individual **nutrients**, they enter your bloodstream through the villi. Next, your blood carries these nutrients to where they are needed.

For example, your brain cells may need some B vitamins to remember all this information. The scrape on your knee may need vitamin K to help it heal. Or, your legs may get energy from carbohydrates, a basic food element. Now you can rush to your next class!

Food spends between three and six hours in the small intestine. The amount of time depends on what the food is made of. For instance, most starchy foods are easily digested and quickly absorbed. Foods that are high in fat and protein take more work. For example, a burger and french fries move at a snail's pace.

Vitamin K is necessary for blood clotting. The body produces its own vitamin K. But, this vitamin is also found in cauliflower and green leafy vegetables, such as cabbage and spinach.

THE LARGE INTESTINE

Not all food parts can be broken down and absorbed. These undigested food parts continue on to the large intestine. It is called large because it is wider than the small intestine. The large intestine is about five feet (2 m) long. Both the large intestine and the small intestine are squished into your **abdomen**.

The large intestine is divided into four parts. These are the cecum, the colon, the rectum, and the anal canal. The main section is the colon. It wraps around the outside of your small intestine like a frame. The colon's main job is to absorb water from undigested food and to store **fecal** matter.

Feces moves to the rectum when the body is ready to rid itself of this material. The solid waste stays in the rectum until you are ready to push it out of the anal canal. Strong muscles, the internal and external **sphincters**, keep the waste in until you tell them to relax.

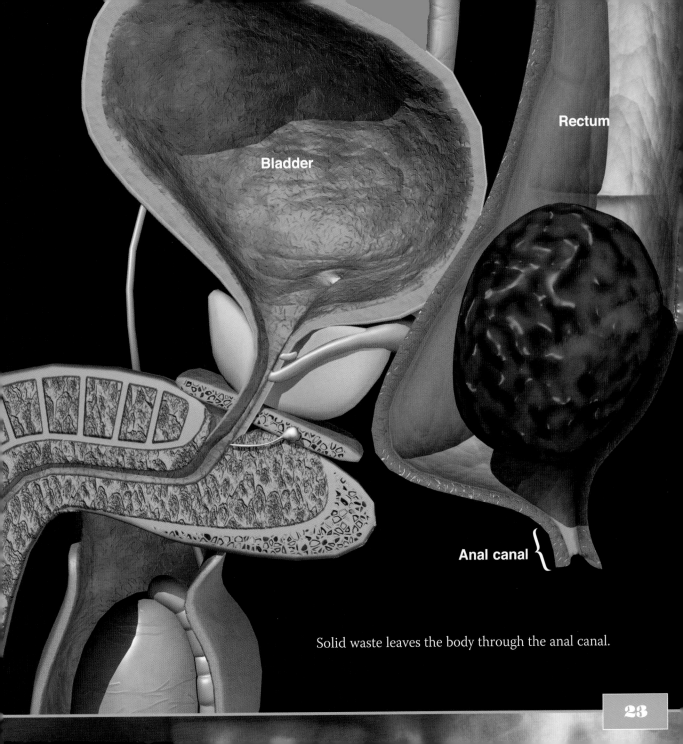

Rectum

Bladder

Anal canal {

Solid waste leaves the body through the anal canal.

YOUR LUNCH'S JOURNEY

It's time to put all this information together. Think of your favorite food. It could be tacos, pizza, or apple pie. Now, let's follow that food's journey through your digestive system from start to finish. Just thinking about your favorite treat may already have your mouth watering. Is your stomach growling, too?

Your mouth "watering" is extra saliva that will start the breakdown of starchy foods. Farther down, your stomach wakes up. It releases an early shot of digestive juices in preparation for food.

Now, take a bite. Yum! After your teeth and tongue have done their work, the esophagus rolls the bolus down. Next stop, the acidic bath of your stomach. Protein digestion begins as your stomach mixes the food around.

Now your food is chyme. Chyme squirts at a steady rate into the small intestine. **Enzymes** from the intestinal walls, the pancreas, and the gallbladder continue to break it down. Villi grab at **nutrients** when they are small enough to pass into your blood vessels. From there, the tiny **nutrients** travel to where they are needed.

However, undigested matter continues on to the large intestine. The colon absorbs extra water and makes the waste more solid. Slowly, solid waste moves toward the anal canal to exit the body. At last! Your favorite food's journey is complete.

Digestion breaks down food, which gives you the energy needed to keep moving!

BURPS AND FARTS!

Burp! Some people burp on purpose. But, everyone burps whether they want to or not. When you eat, drink, and talk, you swallow air. Air is made of gases such as nitrogen and oxygen.

When there is too much air inside of your body, it needs to get out. Extra gas often comes back out of the stomach the way it went in, and you burp. Burping is no big deal, but be sure to say "excuse me!"

Sometimes, extra gas doesn't escape through your mouth. It may move on to your intestines

Too much air in a baby's stomach can cause stomach pains. To avoid this, a baby should be burped once during a feeding and once after the feeding.

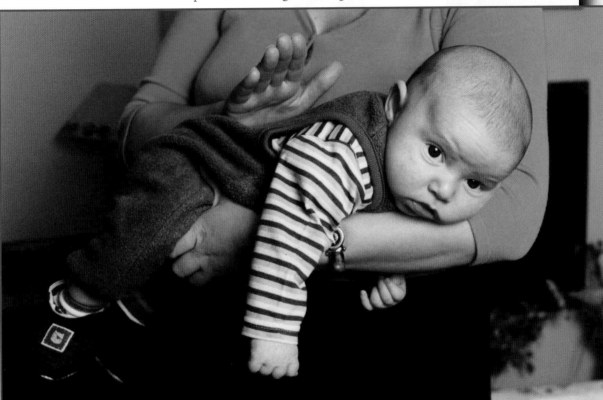

and come out as a fart. Don't worry, everybody farts. However, if you feel uncomfortably gassy, you may need to make some changes in your diet. Eating less pork, beans, and onions may help. And again, just say "excuse me."

OUCH!

Sometimes, your stomach or another part of your digestive system just doesn't feel right. Stomachaches and other pain can happen for many reasons. Eating too much can make you miserable. Even stress can cause digestive problems, such as **indigestion**.

When your tummy hurts, take it easy. If you feel sick or have pain after certain foods, tell an adult. A doctor can help determine if you have a food allergy.

To keep your digestive system in good working order, eat a variety of healthy foods. Fiber is especially important. It is found in whole grain breads, fruits, and vegetables. Fiber prevents **constipation**.

The next time you sit down to eat, think about what's going on inside your body. Thank your teeth, your rumbling stomach, and your intestines. They are always hard at work for you!

Opposite page: The U.S. Department of Agriculture recommends eating a lot of whole grains, fruits, and vegetables. The dietary guidelines also suggest including lean meats, poultry, fish, beans, eggs, and nuts in your diet. Fats are necessary, but they should be limited.

GLOSSARY

abdomen - the part of the body located between the chest and the legs.

automatic - something that happens by itself, without anyone's control.

constipation - a condition marked by difficult or infrequent bowel movements.

diameter - the distance across the middle of an object, such as a circle.

elastic - capable of recovering original size or shape after being stretched, twisted, or squeezed.

enzyme - a complex protein produced in the living cells of all plants and animals. It is used in many of the body's functions, from digestion to clotting.

fecal - of or relating to solid bodily waste.

gastric - of or relating to the stomach.

hormone - a chemical messenger that helps regulate activities in the body.

indigestion - difficulty or discomfort while digesting something.

ingest - to take into the body for digestion.

nutrient - a substance found in food and used in the body to promote growth, maintenance, and repair.

organ - a part of an animal or a plant that is composed of several kinds of tissues and that performs a specific function. The heart, liver, gallbladder, and intestines are organs of an animal.

sphincter - a circular band of muscle that surrounds a body opening. It expands to open and contracts to close the opening.

SAYING IT

amylase - A-muh-lays

carbohydrate - kahr-boh-HEYE-drayt

cecum - SEE-kuhm

chyme - KIME

duodenum - doo-uh-DEE-nuhm

epiglottis - eh-puh-GLAH-tuhs

esophagus - ih-SAH-fuh-guhs

ileum - IH-lee-uhm

jejunum - jih-JOO-nuhm

lipase - LEYE-pays

peristalsis - pehr-uh-STAWL-suhs

pharynx - FA-rihnks

sphincter - SFIHNGK-tuhr

WEB SITES

To learn more about the digestive system, visit ABDO Publishing Company on the World Wide Web at www.abdopublishing.com. Web sites about the human body are featured on our Book Links page. These links are routinely monitored and updated to provide the most current information available.

INDEX